Daniel And The Spanish Robot

The Spanish Café

It was a hot sunny afternoon and Daniel's friends came round for a drink.

The Spanish robot led them into the garden and told them to pretend they were ordering a drink in a lovely outside Spanish café.

The Spanish robot pretended to be a waiter:

The Spanish robot told them that there were the following drinks:

 **una limonada**

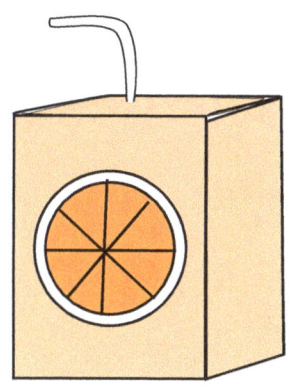 **un zumo de naranja**

 **un zumo de manzana**

Daniel had seen they also had coke, so he whispered to his friends that there was also:

 **una coca cola**

Emily ordered in Spanish a lemonade:

Mathew ordered in Spanish an orange juice:

And Daniel ordered in Spanish a coke:

The Spanish robot went away and came back with:

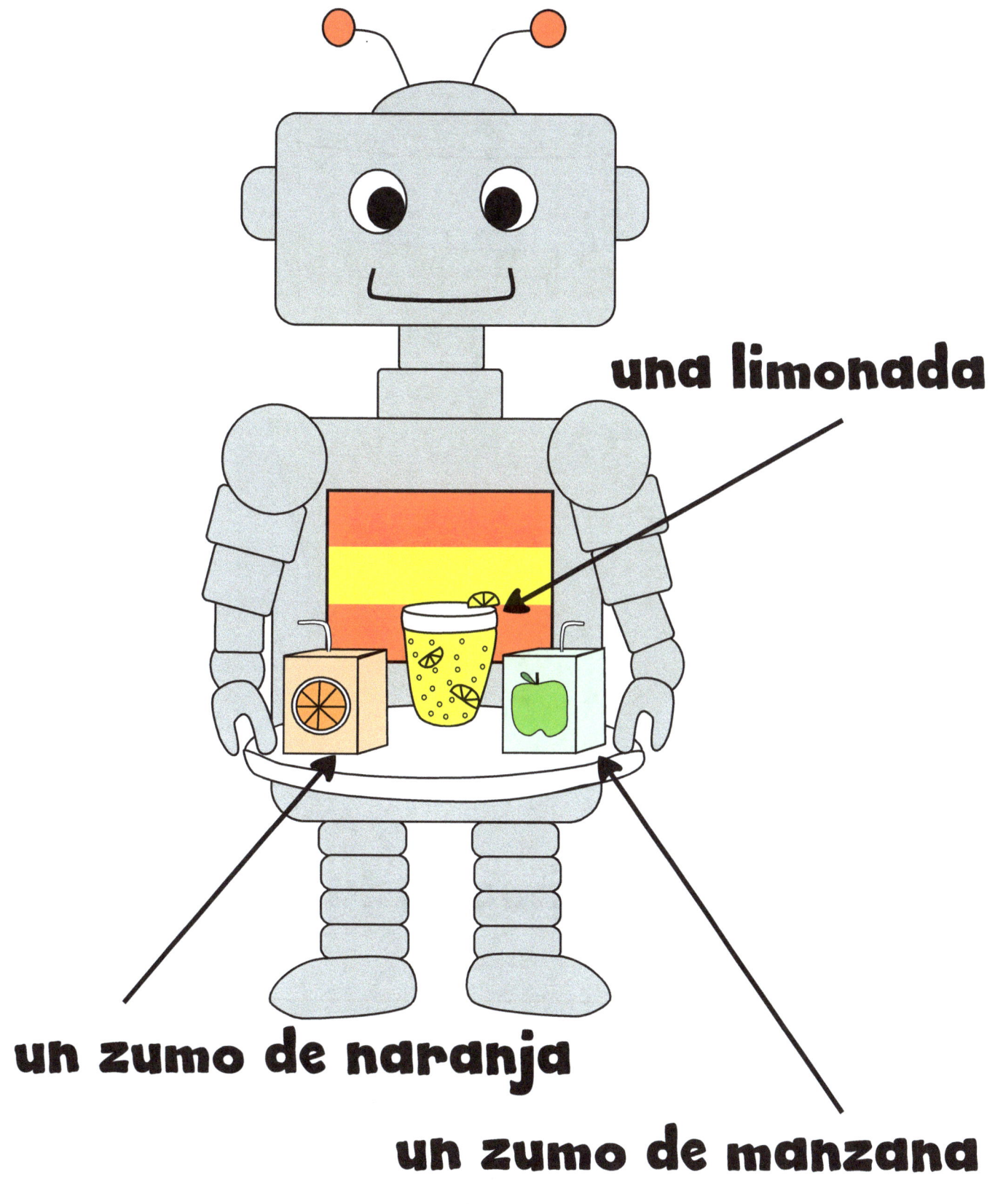

But had he got the drinks order right?

una limonada

Una limonada ..... now that was for Emily.

un zumo de naranja

Un zumo de naranja …. now that was for Matthew.

un zumo de manzana

Emily had **una limonada**.

Matthew had **un zumo de naranja**.

And Daniel had ordered **una coca cola** NOT **un zumo de manzana**!

una coca cola

Una coca cola … now **una coca cola** was for Daniel. Daniel knew it wasn't as healthy as a fruit juice, but he hadn't had **una coca cola** for a while.

They drank their drinks, then Daniel asked for the bill in Spanish:

La cuenta, por favor.

Cinco euros, por favor.

uno dos tres cuatro cinco

They paid the five euro bill with some toy euros they had.

It had been such a fun afternoon!

Can you remember all the drinks we saw?
Let's say them together in Spanish!

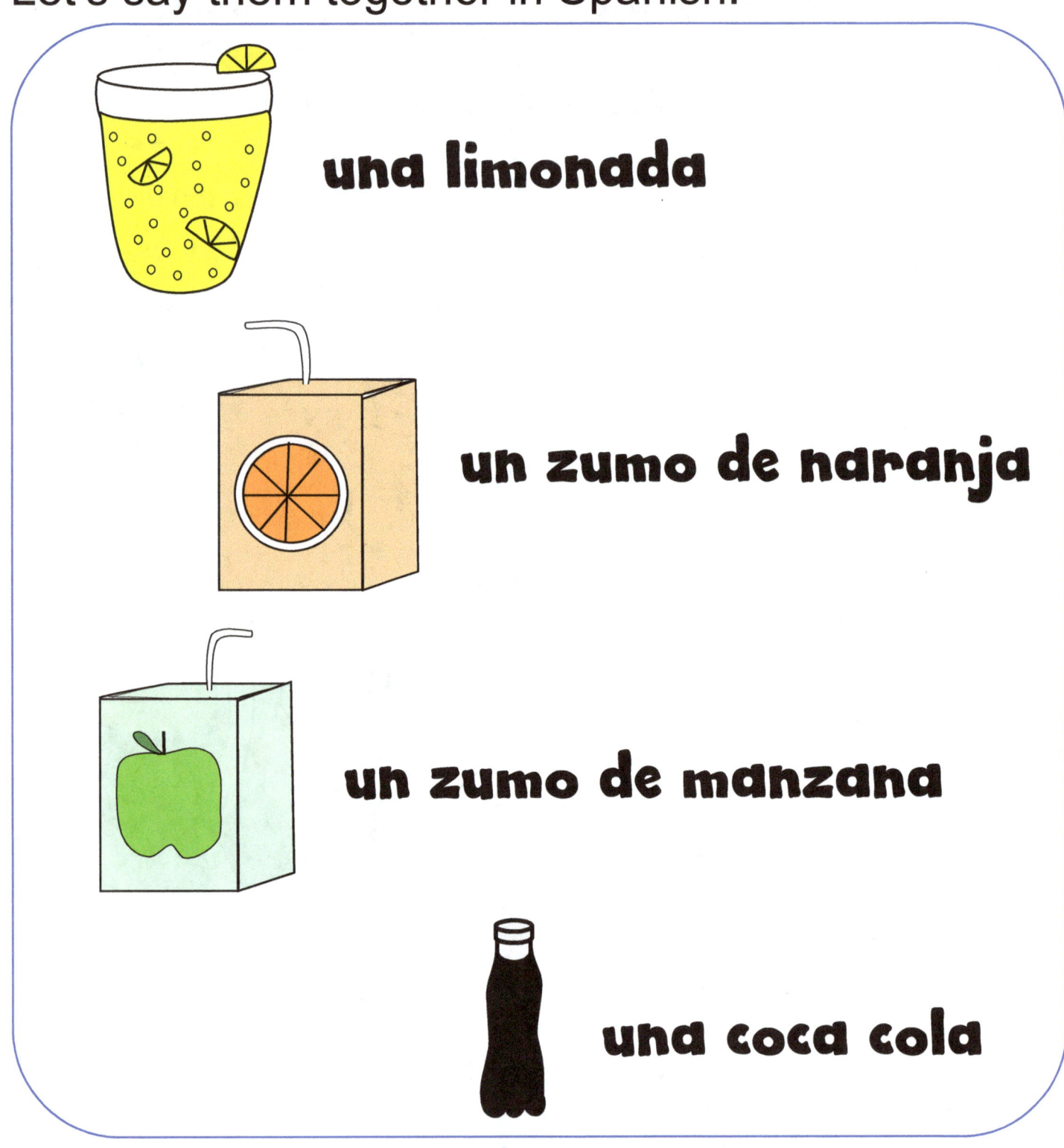

It was time to go home so they all said "**Adiós**".

Daniel And The Spanish Robot

Daniel's Hobbies

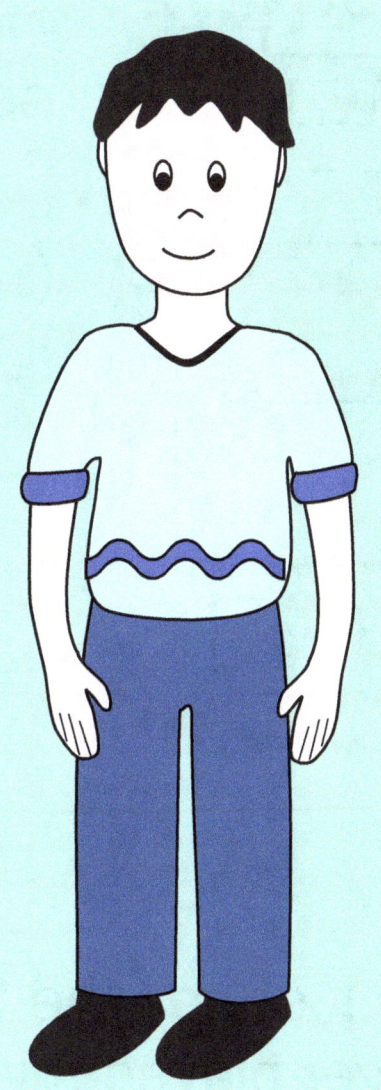

After a few minutes, the Spanish robot decided he liked playing mini-golf so he told Daniel:

They then decided to play football. And the Spanish robot told Daniel he liked football:

They ended up playing football together until they were both very tired!

Now, there's something about reading that the robot really liked. All those fascinating stories and all those interesting facts, so he told Daniel:

They read together for a long time as they were having so much fun.

Daniel liked swimming, so he told the robot:

"Me gusta nadar."

Daniel thought that swimming was so much fun! The robot though didn't say he liked it!

"No me gusta nadar."

Daniel wanted to know why the robot didn't like swimming:

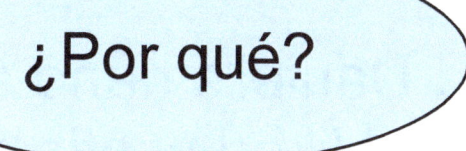

¿Por qué?

So the robot told him about the time he went swimming and he went rusty afterwards as he's made of metal!

The Spanish robot liked skating. Daniel had got some boots with wheels on a while ago but he had found it hard. Maybe it was time to try them again!

The Spanish robot held Daniel's hand and showed him how to skate. Daniel liked skating, so he told the Spanish robot:

Me gusta patinar.

After a while it began to rain, so they went inside.

The Spanish robot asked Daniel if he liked singing:

¿Te gusta cantar?

Daniel liked singing, so he replied:

Me gusta cantar.

They switched on the radio, and sang lots of songs together. They sang together until Daniel was called for his dinner.

Daniel had told the Spanish robot about the hobbies he liked. Let's say together in Spanish what he'd said:

They liked a lot of the same things! It was a shame though that robots rust in water as Daniel liked swimming. Maybe he could get a special waterproof suit made for robots. What do you think? **¿Te gusta nadar?** (Do YOU like to swim?)

Spanish - English word list

Useful Spanish words

Hola - - - - - - - - - - - - - - - - - - - Hello
Adiós - - - - - - - - - - - - - - - - - - Good bye
Sí - Yes
No - No
Por favor - - - - - - - - - - - - - - - - Please
Gracias - - - - - - - - - - - - - - - - - Thank you

1	uno (one)
2	dos (two)
3	tres (three)
4	cuatro (four)
5	cinco (five)

Drinks

una limonada
(a lemonade)

un zumo de naranja
(an orange juice)

una coca cola
(a coke)

un zumo de manzana
(an apple juice)

Hobbies

Me gusta (I like)   No me gusta (I don't like)

el mini-golf
(mini-golf)

el fútbol
(football)

nadar
(swimming)

leer
(reading)

cantar
(singing)

patinar
(skating)

Let's sing a song!

The following words could either be sung to a made up tune, or you could try saying the words as a rap.

For inspiration of a melody to use you could hum first a nursery rhyme. How many different versions can you create using the lyrics?

una limonada, una limonada
por favor, por favor
una limonada, una limonada
por favor, por favor

una coca cola, una coca cola
por favor, por favor
una coca cola, una coca cola
por favor, por favor

un zumo de naranja, un zumo de naranja
por favor, por favor
un zumo de naranja, un zumo de naranja
por favor, por favor

un zumo de manzana, un zumo de manzana
por favor, por favor
un zumo de manzana, un zumo de manzana
por favor, por favor

Now pretend to order a drink in a lovely outside Spanish café! One person will be the waiter / waitress and one person will be the customer. You can change una limonada to a different drink if you want to.

Waiter / Waitress: Hola
Customer: Una limonada, por favor
Waiter / Waitress: Una limonada   *(Pretend to hand over the drink the customer orders)*
Customer: Gracias

© Joanne Leyland 2017   2018   Second edition 2021
The word list and the song lyrics may be photocopied by the purchasing institution or teacher for class or home use. The story may not be photocopied or reproduced digitally without the prior written agreement of the author.

www.ingramcontent.com/pod-product-compliance
Lightning Source LLC
Chambersburg PA
CBHW081359080526
44588CB00016B/2548